© Copyright 2019, All rights reserved.

The content contained within this book may not be reproduced, duplicated or transmitted without direct written permission from the author or the publisher.

Under no circumstances will any blame or legal responsibility be held against the publisher, or author, for any damages, reparation, or monetary loss due to the information contained within this book; either directly or indirectly.

Legal Notice:

This book is copyright protected. This book is only for personal use. You cannot amend, distribute, sell, use, quote or paraphrase any part, or the content within this book, without the consent of the author or publisher.

Disclaimer Notice:

Please note the information contained within this document is for educational and entertainment purposes only. All effort has been executed to present accurate, up to date, and reliable, complete information. No warranties of any kind are declared or implied. Readers acknowledge that the author is not engaging in the rendering of legal, financial, medical or professional advice.

FOREWARD

Briana and I met during my second year at university. Ever since day one, it was apparent that poetry was her passion. Through her writing and publishing endeavors to live performances, poetry was an essential part of her education. She has a gift, and that was clear to me when I was given the chance to read her work. It is as if the writing came from her very soul. I could feel each emotion, visualize each scenario, and find meaning in every word. Her writing is a reflection of who she is as a person; brilliant, passionate, and caring. Somehow she is able to connect with each reader, and allow you to see and understand her perspective. Being able to see the world through her eyes has not only been a unique experience for me, but has also been a welcome and thoughtful gift. I hope it feels the same for each of you.

-Charlotte Weisman

Acknowledgements

I would like to thank my friends and family for loving me, supporting me, and being yourselves with me. Thank you to my editor Grace Gabriella Puskas for enriching my words with your expertise. I also would like to thank my contributors and friends Thessa Andrade, Treina Santos, and Dominique Durden; I am always taken by your writing. Thank you to Alice Walker, Zora Neale Hurston, James Baldwin, and the symphony of Black writers and intellectuals who have gone before me. Thank you for writing your words that have validated me and gave me the freedom to write my own. Lastly, thank you to my teachers, mentors, aunties, cousins, pastors, and all of the women who have taken me under their wings and nurtured me.

You're helping me grow into a woman I am proud of.

There is something here for you. Whoever you are, know that you are worthy. There is healing in love, in your lowest moments, in your triumphs. You are worthy of creating a life for yourself before anyone else.

And another thing, I dedicate this book to the college professor that said inner city kids have nothing to say worth listening to. Buy my book luv

✧Contents✧

✧The Roots:

✧The Undoing:

✧The Restoration:

✧The Flourish:

Art/ Illustrations Index

The Creation of the First Witch

She is pulled from rib,
the first cage she'd ever seen
with her own eyes.

She is-
the shadow no one wants to follow (them) by day.
Woman---the pillows they whisper to at night.
She is a witch because she's too good at rhyming,
she is everywhere and keeps perfect timing.
You would think she was the first woman with beginnings in her hands
while the endings wait in her peripherals.
They say she is omnipresent,
She says tired.
They call her sorceress-
she says only when tempted.
They say burn her at the stake
and she insists she was born there.
But she is glad they finally see her
and take her name for records,
now her existence is on record
and it can only be debated by time and who's history survives.
But she is here-
and she knows it isn't conjured magic,
it's divine grace.

God's Sister

Blood bonds, and it bridges space and time;
blood ain't the only thing keeping us
anymore.
We choose to be keepers.
We choose to be ourselves together.
We know everything except for the future
and what makes woman, not man,
and who's the god our daddy serves?
Does he look like me?
Does he have a sister that he love like me,
and does she smile like she shouldn't?
like the secret is dirty?
Does daddy's god see girls whose secrets are dirty?
Whose fingers stick to everything she tried to leave at the cross
Can she touch his hem, then?
Can I still touch him if he isn't near me,
but She is.

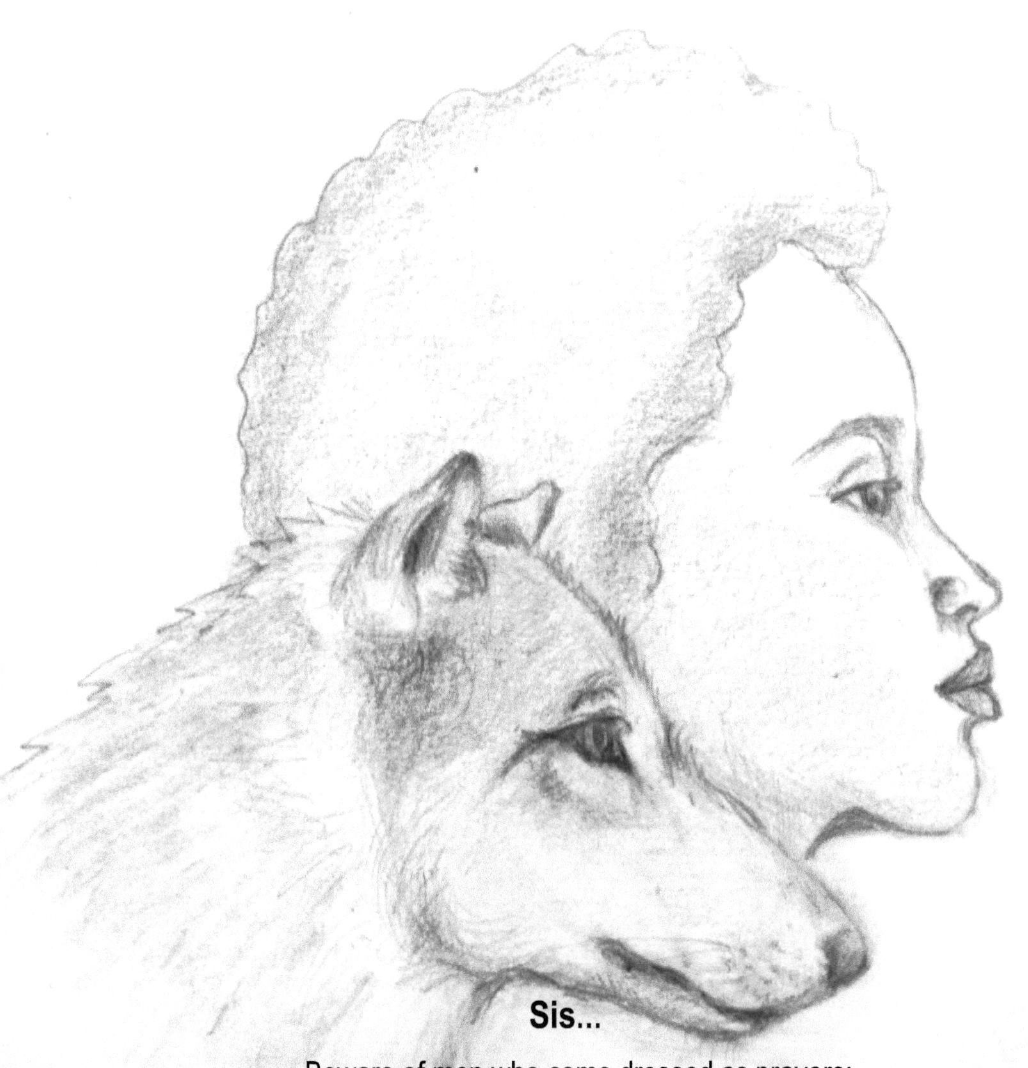

Sis...

Beware of men who come dressed as prayers;
they consume you under full moons, their
affections change with the tides.
They are wolves.
They dance with dazzling ruby teeth and killer's intent.
Your pearls will become their prize.

The Undoing

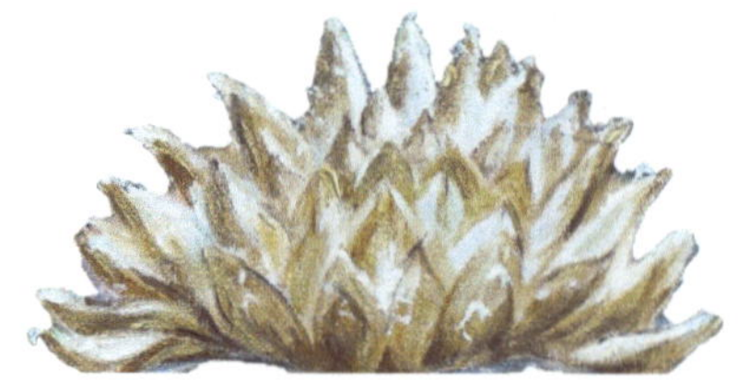

The Gardens We've Tended

Broken trust is a weed,
no one truly knows when it's planted;
over time it is watered and cultivated
with idle space for interpretation.
They intertwine with flowers like lover's hands,
they size up peonies for devouring, like snakes;
they turn rose bushes to thorns,
herbs to forgotten rot, and hard work to lost potential.
Memories crackle and hiss into ashes,
Ashes settle in the lungs of the new generation;
until everything is broken.
Your world is dry,
and the person you knew
isn't there to witness these undoings.

A Family that Balances on Knives

A lot can happen in a moment.
A lot can happen in a kitchen,
where the food chain is set and maintained.
Resentment is served cold on the china,
While our arguing bounces off the dull knives that still cut when need be.
Reason is left toppling over and spilling out of the cabinets,
Into a pot of rage that bubbles over.
We don't eat at tables that often turn on us.
Indifference smiles in our family pictures.
We don't know each other by the way we love,
We know we're family by how we bruise.
The wounds peek under thin dermis, ready to surface at any moment.
We tear at the flesh we share, eager to find out if blood runs longer than history.
Maybe we can bury these demons in our memories--- the Egypt we never go back to.
As you back me into corners filled with your monsters,
You yell at me, and I'm vaguely aware that I didn't turn off the tea...
It's as hot as your blood on the side of my face.
I cut you and it's always an accident,
when mom comes I convince her it's always an accident.
She says I'm clumsy and forgetful,
and I leave things on the burner too long.
But we put our anger on the back burner,
no wonder we burn each other when the steam screams
and the fire alarms roar.
I never seem to forget these floors,
or the holes in the door,
or the walls,
places in my home my blood knows, it boils at the thought.
I am always at war with someone who fights with my fears held to my neck
that we will test each other's wounds until they run deeper than we remember,
where we call houses homes without each other,
But we are all we have.
We've been fighting in spirit longer than our bodies have documented the blows.
God spilled His son's blood all over the page,
But only I am bleeding.
He forgot to turn off His kettle, and take it off the eye.
A lot can happen in that moment God took His eyes off me.

What to Get the Person Who Has Given You Nothing but Trauma for Christmas

Maybe a scarf.
A scarf will protect your neck from the cold,
or maybe it can mask the lump that forms in my throat when I see you.
We can't spell family with fear, but we use it to hold ours together,
maybe we can use it to decorate the tree, the last living thing left in our living room.
Living rooms encase these dead things with trimmings.

Maybe I'll give you time.
Another Christmas to open gifts and wounds alike
Another Christmas where I give each paper cut and each callous its own monologue
Together wounds and I groan as one chorus
We praise the power to cauterize under pressure; we cut off and store these dead things for later.

Why get something for someone you don't like?
Because maybe the absence of the gift is the acknowledgement of their violence.
Because maybe we can't afford to bring the gravity of that pain into the one holiday we spend so much on ignoring,
just so we can dodge eye contact,
and smile with daggers and not with our teeth.
Just so we can look at the photos next year,
and say that was a good year.

I've wrestled with how to write your name on this wrapping paper,
I struggle with seeing you smile, and knowing that vengeance is the Lord's.
But She ain't gotta sit across from you,
she ain't gotta pass off involuntary flinching as hugs,
or keep the family close when we have been thrown across sea beds of resentment.
All She knows is everything,
and all my wounds know is time to feel your smile against my gauze.
Maybe I'll give you my tears again.
Maybe I'll give you all the reasons I can't stomach the thought of trusting a man.
And all the ghosts of their names spill out like a broken dam
But it starts with you.
Maybe I'll give you forgiveness for Christmas and save myself the money.
One day.

Monster by Thessa Andrade

Sometimes I wonder why I am the way I am,
I blame it on the exposure, hoping I find closure,
while reflecting my composure.
But it doesn't feel like I get any closer, so more of these desperate emotions take over-
the ones that repeat without a consistent beat, you know, that immediately
come back just by the sound of "are you okay?"
The response you can't erase on your face.
No matter how much your smudge or try to displace with hate,
people know better.
And then you wish you were better...
at excuses,
but you know you hurt like war
and cry more than a river;
you can't seem to keep the liquor out-
out of your liver.
That's how You cope-
hope. You hope they have become the same thing so you cope
and hope for a better tomorrow.
But you can't seem to see tomorrow,
all you can see is the emptiness of the bottle, and how it matches the emptiness of my heart.
If that dropped too, it would shatter and no longer piece together smoothly with its
parts.
I am the undesirable-
no positive adjectives match my character,
I am no person worthy of attaching to ideas
and story lines that make people go to sleep at night.
Matter of fact, I will be
the nightmare you see during the day.

I Smoke When I Wanna Make Love

I smoke when I wanna make love to our memories
perched on the shelf inside of me,
collecting the years.
Never collecting dust because I revisit too often,
everytime I roll up, it's another smoky haze where
I see us, like it was yesterday.
Or I kissed you and woke up to your scent earlier today.
You say you'll be in the same place when I get home
and I think it's funny the past and I call home the same place,
the place where we groan and stretch after long days;
make messes and remind ourselves to clean when they get in our way...
Get into bed and savor shedding our skins,
we find rest and wake up to the sameness
just to roll over and up again.
"*To us*," I say, as we look each other in the eyes
or seven more years of bad sex.

A History of Love in My Family

The women in my family have the best recipes,
But they couldn't scrape love's absence from their teeth.
They'd say a good meal is the way to a man's heart,
But his respect is nestled next to his pride,
and under his pride are where his secrets lie.
Never ask a man what's in his closet, *baby don't you know?*
He can be the only one closest to his skeletons
And Love doesn't live with scary things in the closet.
Love is not haunted,
But we are the haunted.
We made homes for these bones,
and all we have to show are graves and calloused hands.
We hold on to dreams that fester more than they manifest.

My grandmother died, never having been in love.
And I think my heart broke.
My biggest fear is not being loved for my truth.
Only being desired in my youth, and as time crawls and drips,
the dust settles:
People settle with whatever truth they'd laid with since.
And I am still misunderstood,
And I am still in waiting,
My heart runs out of words to fill time with infinite rhymes,
and I run out of space on the lines.
With nothing to anchor them to.
No scent that brings these words to the back of my throat,
And no joy to remind my smile which way it should go.
What if my generational curse is loneliness?
Is love lost?
How do I love then?
How do I love when I was born with a chip on my shoulder that belonged to my mother and her mother before her?
How do I love when my body has been a warring zone more than it's been Holy Grail?
How do I love you when love means we look each other in the eyes when we fight?
Tell me, how someone armors up to fight the world,
find love, and not have it reflect my shortcomings.

My grandmother died, never having been in love.
And I know it broke my heart.
Knowing that black women die every day, being praised for the love we give
And brave enough to live despite the love we don't receive in return.

I am tired of love with no return.
Of lessons with no memories.
Of being love's waiting room.
And scars that make the ugly—picturesque.
My grandma died, never having been in love.
Even though she was loved.
And I think it broke her heart.
To not know how to receive it.
To not know she was worth it.
Where are the recipes that take the bitterness out of that?

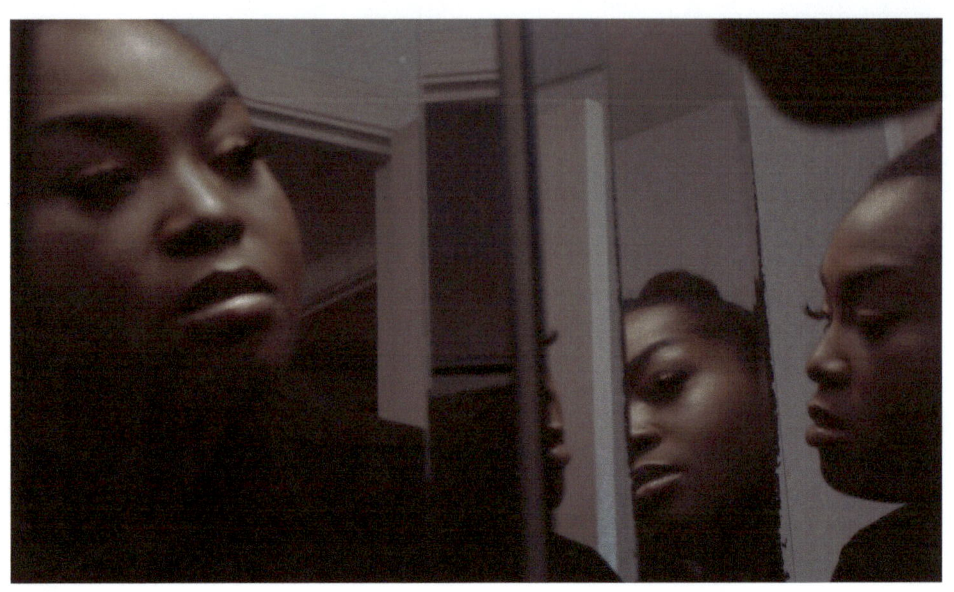

The Restoration

She lifts my chin and looks into me

like an empty store window.

She is searching for the opening hour-

she thought she knew.

She smells the gunpowder and tears in my pores

and begs me to come home,

from war with myself.

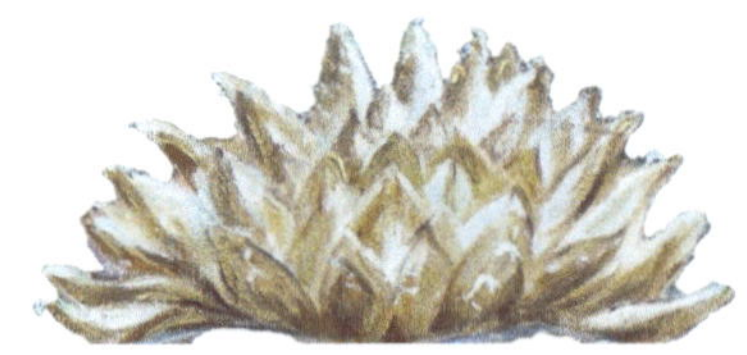

The Process (to a Promise of Healing)

I don't know how to write a survivor's poem.
Maybe it sounds like anger, or splintered glass.
I don't know how to write his sins when I feel ashamed and I know I shouldn't be,
but tell me how you feel when your attacker walks free-
like ghosts in the goonies.
I don't know how to write from a place where the wild things haunt me,
there will always be someone there to say he was a boy; who does what boys do,
like steal your toys,
pull your hair,
or hold you by the throat when you're gasping for air.

He was a smooth talker,
dressed in a suit he was a loaded gun walking-
the type of brother that made you ask your mother:
How did you know you met daddy?
How did you know he could hold your sugar like caddies?
What tipped you off that he was worth the risk, and if your risk caught you by the wrist, how did you know you were in danger?
How did you know out of the sweetest fruit he was the stranger?
And you'd end up bitter, with the most elusive ideas of love throbbing the scars he left you.
How was I supposed to know he'd leave me hollow in my own body with nothing to come home to?
Momma, teach me to know demons from how easily they come and how evil they laugh as they play with you.

I am ashamed I wanted him to want me,
although I knew he lacked the understanding to make him a man,
I made myself into something that lies slack.
He wiped transgressions on my skin and claimed me dirty,
and named me aggressive.
Like all of the bullets in woman's temple,
He does not pray to the God of my temple.
Maybe there's a heaven for women's agency,
Maybe there is a hell for men's supremacy.
I'd be the first one to send him to the flames he's ignited in me.
Hell hath no fury like a woman harmed, and my god,
She believes in reciprocity.

I don't know how to write a survivor's poem.
Maybe it sounds like healing on a bad day.
The spot on my floor where I hold myself together is dampened with rivers of tears.
My voice stutters like disbelief,

and my thoughts burn and blend violently.
I bend at the waist, waiting for answers,
waiting for God to lift me by my chin and call me by my healing, and not by his shame.
Some nights that voice never answers,
some nights it whispers how I am not alone and pain does not define me.
But his anger seems to find me and confine me to this memory
as he says he will have a black queen with some black ass kids,
while I am reduced to pink matter between the floor and him;
the spine to hold up his dream of the perfect woman he'd never disrespect.
He'd never hold her like me...
Maybe she was worthy.

There are holes in me that match the shape of his hands.
In them, he holds all the forgiveness he does not deserve.
All the forgiveness I haven't been able to spare.
All the forgiveness I must give~
to myself.

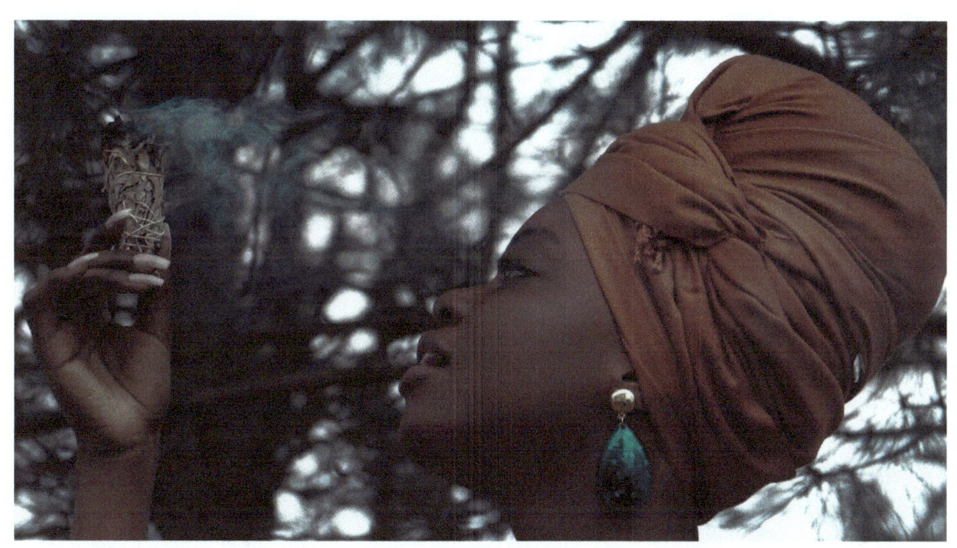

Again by Treina Santos

Leaves unfurling,
I'm expanding.
Past traumas- growing pains;
I'm deciding
it's time to bloom.

Remembering Innocence

Do you ever look at clouds anymore,
imagine anymore? Do you remember innocence?
When there were vivid hues, waving birds, and flags that stood for you-
Do you remember being born?
The wombs formed from wounds, bending and morphing and cracking
to bring your first breath from hushed prayers.
Do you remember the day you first felt human?
The gradual sting of humanity that slowly fastened your feet onto the ground,
until they felt like sidewalks. The day clouds became scientists and not metaphors for the other.
Your mother takes off her crown at the kitchen table when you're supposed to be sleeping;
and your father scrapes his manhood from the dirt on his construction boots by the door.
You wait for them to swell and become superheroes---instead they shrink further.

Do you remember when love was a holy friend,
instead of holes in your favorite jeans after you fell for them?
Did you feel the friendship shifting under your eyes when you kissed for the first time?
What made you not cower and shrink from love, the first time?
The prick of your finger, now scabbed and unrecognizable, was the first time you saw how you bleed when you picked up the pieces of hearts that were broken by yours.
Does your soul shiver with the memories of the first time?
How your spirits saw eye to eye, and the smooth parts of your mind prickled against his clawed flaws. You caressed and he pressed; and knew then,
that love was a balancing act best done alone.
Did you look at the moon that night?
Is that when you stopped seeing a face in the craters, like cartoons before the static?
Do you still look at the clouds? And see, your innocence kicking their legs,
waving, watching, and waiting, for your remembrance?

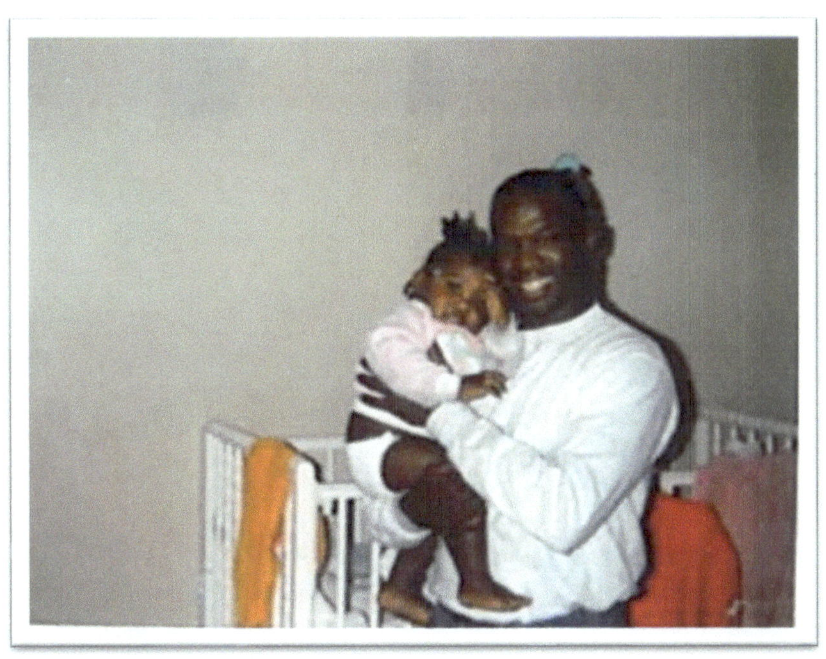

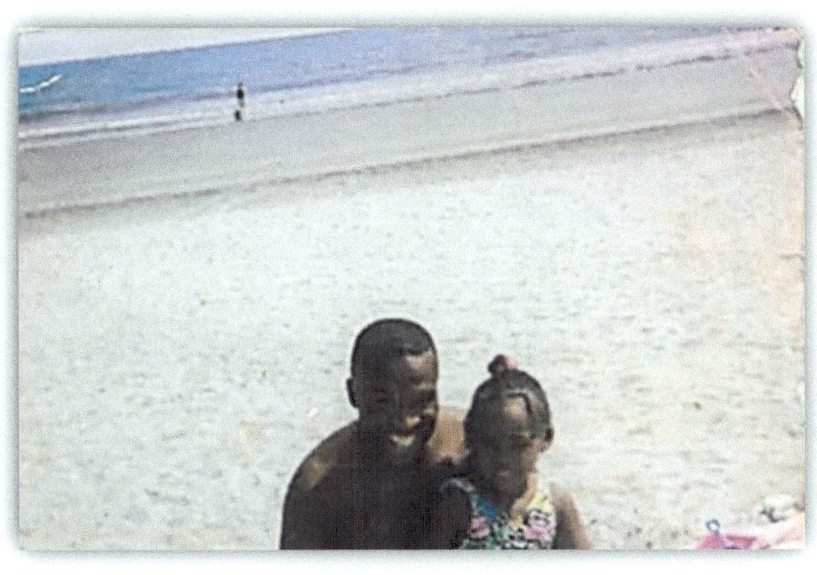

Dear Dad

Somewhere inside I think I remember your face, it reminds me of mine.
You are deep in the trenches of the girl, I rarely am anymore.
I remember your bowed-legged walk.
I still catch your scent cowering in the seams of your fishing hat.
I can't hear you say my name anymore, it was the first thing I remember forgetting.
I've folded this consciousness into a secret and shelved you.

My thoughts of you are voodoo dolls.
I poke them and they growl at me, trapped in another life, a "what if" time.
What if I learned how to ride my bike with you?
What if you taught me how to cut and scar?
What if I learned my worth through you?

I learned how to live in the land of what ifs, because you're my dad there.
You meet all my boyfriends, and tell me they're terrible for me.
They never deserve me, and I believe them the first time they show me they're unworthy.
In this reality, there are less scars to count.
Your wedding band is on your aging fingers where it still means forever.
And we walk down the aisle, my hand confidently nestled in yours.
In this reality, I have love I don't have to perform for.

I think your absence has taught me enough.
I've learned to love people by the way they leave me.
Constantly appreciating retreating figures where these soul ties swing like hammocks between us.
There's always something tip toeing in the balance between us;
So I've learned to call it grace.
In this reality, I give too many chances.
In this reality, there are too many graves to count, and too many spiritual realms for heaven to make sense.

I am scared to commit to being left one day.
I don't want to have to sew the good memories into my child's mind like hand-me-downs;
like my mother did.
She is the wife of a memory, and I am fathered by potential and nostalgia.
No wonder I date men who make me feel like your absence does-
it reminds me of the girl, I rarely am anymore.

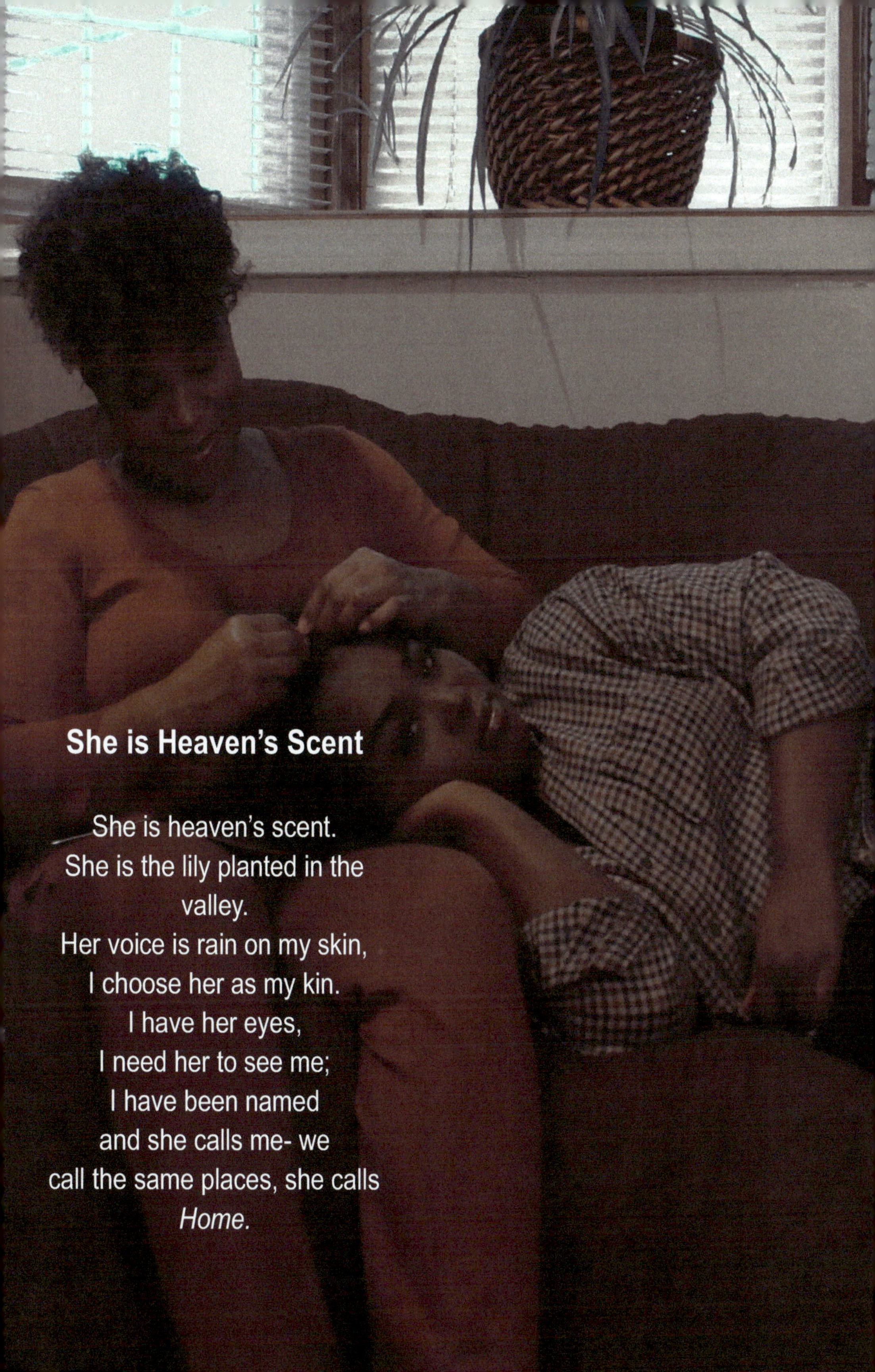

She is Heaven's Scent

She is heaven's scent.
She is the lily planted in the
valley.
Her voice is rain on my skin,
I choose her as my kin.
I have her eyes,
I need her to see me;
I have been named
and she calls me- we
call the same places, she calls
Home.

Love Vs. the World

They say I am too black to love,
too loud to like;
too ugly to keep in cameras.
But I am still pressed on the walls-
I make them clean.

My body is a house full of hallways,
emptying echoes bounce through my ribcage.
My hunger for home wails and only I can hear it,
only I can sense the rumble in my spirit.
I am praying to a God I haven't felt close to
so I can come home to a love I'm not used to.
The kind that don't see ugly as unfixable
The kind that bend n stretch like good denim
I know it exists,
and I know it doesn't shrink from monsters;
I know it isn't scared to love the biggest blackest hole in the room
and to tell me to smile,
or tell me to bite...
Love tells me to bear my teeth though the world says it's ugly,
and they're right.
Because ladies loving themselves ain't ladylike,
As the world's hate turns into wine under my feet
I take a sip and thank God for the bitter becoming sweet
In due time; we learn to smile and toast to baring our teeth
against the ugly.
Together, we shrink it into the walls
to watch and observe my homecoming.
She calls me- we
call the same places,
home.

Aunty Politics

Aunty politics says that breadcrumbs don't go on no Mac n' cheese.
Aunty politics says to fix my little friend a plate before I eat.
Aunty politics says the good days were when women put some clothes on;
Like y'all didn't have freaknik.
Like y'all really "covered up" back then.
Like y'all knew freedom in your womanhood wasn't behind a man's claim to you.
When did you feel like being a woman was the most important thing to prove?
Aunty, why can't I be free to choose?

Choose to be the woman that is seen and heard just as much.
Choose to be the woman who doesn't want to be a woman some times.
Can I be a woman that loves with my needs in mind?
Give me the rights to my life
Let me have love that is *mine*.

Aunty politics says men are gonna be men and I gotta keep 'em feeling like one.
Their presence is meant to change my appearance:
covering up in my own home, avoiding stares that are uninvited.
Aunty politics says he's family, and he's always invited.
Even though he hugs me too much, and strokes hearts in my hand during prayer.

Aunty politics says R Kelly just needs prayer,
They post his bail then shame their daughters.
Swaying to the devil's tunes, while sipping on poisonous juice, inhaling smoke that our bodies shouldn't be used to, but we know where we stand.
Aunty politics still step in the name of love.
Aunty politics tells me pussy in pounds is currency and I still ain't enough-
Aunty politics tells me I am more sin than woman, and blood can't fix what continues to bleed.

Maybe it's jealousy.
Maybe truth skips a generation.
Maybe they carry this curse because they don't trust themselves to be women without restriction.
Maybe they are still living where they were broken.
They give life to the places in them that were policed, shunned, and held for ransom.
Some have never gotten their names back, and they don't know what to call the things they've lost.
These broken women feed us trauma for dinner, hoping to bond in the ways broken girls often do.
They compare scars and bandages, whisper who offended them,
and they're surprised when some names are repeated.
Aunty politics are the rules of these scarred sisters,
They repeat them too often to ever heal.

Ctrl Alt Deleteblkwomxn by Dominique Durden

The women I know used to shrink all the time,
now, we bare our teeth,
and drink the blood of our enemies.
After all, anything that bleeds be unholy-
isn't that why you call us witches?
Call us hysterical,
call me bitch.
Bitch please,
I could swallow you whole in one bite and use your bones to pick my teeth when I'm finished.
Boy, I birthed you;
don't you ever disrespect your mother!
And yeah, Crystal, you were right,
every time I walk into a room
my black goes before me, while my woman sits in the back where she will neither be seen nor heard.
Sometimes my woman walks into the room before me, and locks my Black out because my black is too black, and I'm the only black in the room... my woman cannot afford to be the stereotype;
even though she be angry,
even though she be right,
even though she be backbone, and
even though she is too much of all to only be one.
Still she be forced to choose,
like you can separate one from the other when you are the bastard child of bondage.
My woman closes the door on my black,
my black closes the door on my woman.
My woman and my black fight every single day.
My woman, and my black, be tired.
My woman and my black be so tired because she be everything to everybody and don't get none of the credit for everything she gives.
And she gives,
and gives,
and gives,
until she can't give no more, but then she gives again.
She be the meat, the bone and the marrow.
She be the cook, the pot and everything in the pot,
and still have to clean up everyone else's mess.
And maybe that comes with the territory-
perhaps Medusa was a black woman?

You know how they be demonizing us when we talk back.

Perhaps it wasn't snakes in her hair, but locks,
and if I am my mother's child I have followed in her footsteps.
If there's anything that she has taught me, it's that looks can kill,
and that if I have to serve a man
I should serve him well done.

Miss Sofia's Song

Big breasted, blackened skin, balled fist,
She takes the breath out of this world
And puts it in her bra like a pack of Newports;
She dares science to explain her.

Greeting mountains like pebbles,
Sofia is a sonnet for girls like me.
An independent broken thing.
An edge of a woman that has no guilt about pushing you to your limits.
She says a prayer for your freedom over your happiness,
She prays in time, you'll choose yourself over them both.

All her life Miss Sofia* had to fight.
And I think it's sad that her truth is a punchline.
Every time she had to choose survival over her desire for intimacy,
Every time her eyes refused to shut unless she was ready to die.
She was left swinging wildly,
Untamed and loved because of it.
Taunting any man who would dare try to turn her to dust.
She always had to have someone hold her virtue as if they were earrings,
She be damned if she let her husband black her eye.
She be damned if her brother taught her to bow, before her god did.
She be damned anyways.
She be fighting fire with hell,
And she doesn't tell her god she is tired.

No one likes a black girl that is only human,
No one likes an unwanted thing that insists on existing anyways.
Miss Sofia exists on the outskirts of her skirts where the dirt catches on;
And has the nerve to call it dainty.
She has the nerve to say every scar loses its story, if you get enough of them.

Her laugh forces her smile out of its corner,
Lips peel back like show curtains,
Hips dip and widen to show she is more of a woman than she is given credit for,
She will find her pleasures in this life.
And make whiskey of them in the next.
She will hoot n holler,
Slam her hand on tables,
Swear at the saints,
And tell them to loosen up.
She will tell them persecution has made them soft.

But she is no stranger to battered bones,
And living like her life is the only thing she owns.
It's rare like the pearls her mother gave her,
It's harsh like the truth that she didn't deserve them.
She comes from bitter fruit,
But coming into her sweetness is her greatest rebellion.

*Miss Sofia is a character from The Color Purple by Alice Walker

Ivory Coast Towers (For that Special Dysfunctional Man We All Know Too Well...Or Grow Up to Be)

Ivory Coast tower,
may I grind the commitment out of you
and inherit your insecurities like a common cold.
May I stick around longer than your mother did,
and may I be as irreplaceable as the pain of her neglect,
because she has stained every woman's image in your eyes.
Your misogyny brands us all the same in deep cellars built with your rage.

Tiny men in big shoes-
call me daddy along with your issues;
call me king along with you absence of value.
You are wise with no knowledge of self,
talking a big game- you oversell yourself,
prisoned by your shortcomings. You're in a cell by yourself,
black men need to stand but you still can't stand yourself.
You's a man?
We march for your rights?
Every conversation turns into a pissing contest, call them cock fights,
you always creepin into DMs.
A woman's worst nightmare walks in broad daylight.

Niggas speak up just by stepping on their woman's air pipes,
you need'a become a plumber to learn how to lay down pipe-
you ain't bout shit,
and you ain't worth the hype!
Your hairline still deciding which direction it wanna take in life
but I'm sleep tho,
your woman cries about you and never scream out when she with you-
but I'm sleep tho;
fake deep nigga, you and your words barely a deep throat
yet all the problems are me though?
You say you got an army of hoes;
I don't know how any woman can follow a bust quick general
I'mma salute them, tho...

My nerves tense but my back loose,
you ain't even work it out-
all these problems and stress and
you ain't even worth it now.

Forget who you say you are
cause your name is clown nigga.
While you swearing n' moaning,
I don't make a sound nigga.
Yous a never-there, never-around nigga.
Yous a crusty where-my-hug-at nigga-
you'll never be down.
You'll never get a queen,
so how you figure?
You betta call becky...
Drink some Lemonade nigga.

You're a slave to whipping your own back
just to beat the same dead horse;
all this caring and loving makes me go hoarse.
You will never hear me and digest my words,
Ivory Coast towers are really slave holdings to past molds.
Isn't it a shame your past is all you think you're worth?

The Flourish

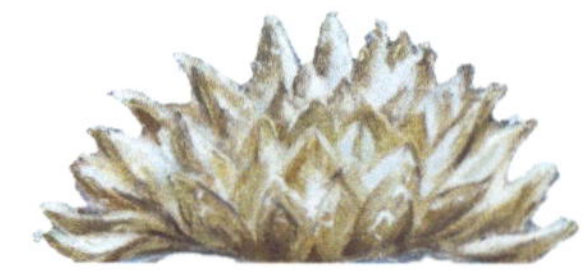

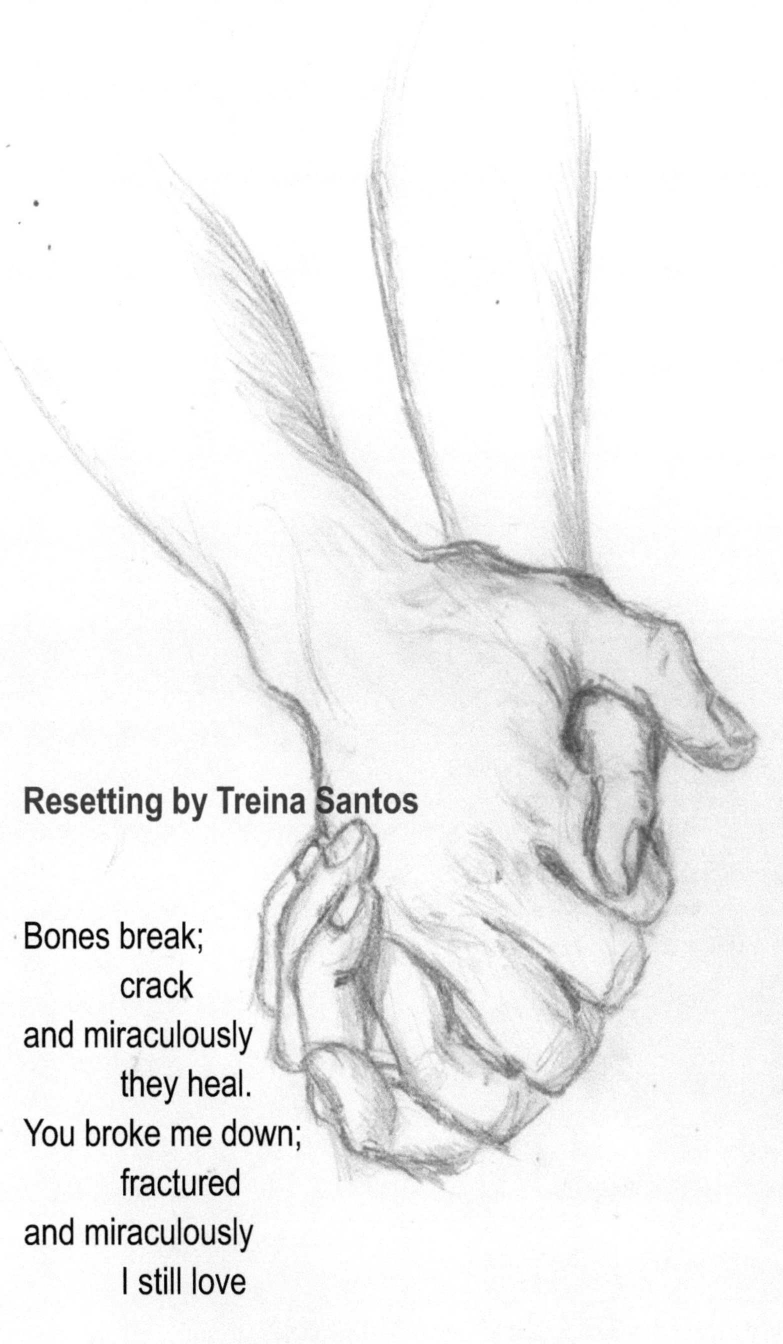

Resetting by Treina Santos

Bones break;
crack
and miraculously
they heal.
You broke me down;
fractured
and miraculously
I still love

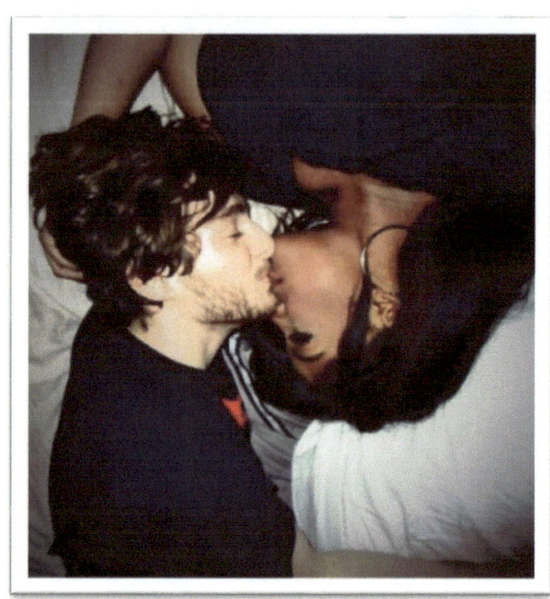

Worshipping Someone with Your Eyes

Before my eyes become too heavy with the bags I'm carrying,
full of souvenirs from their trips,
Let me see you.
Let me take pictures of your physicality mentally,
and take you in like a baby's first breath on the outside.

Your body language croons decibels,
thick fingers give me flashbacks of what is yet,
sandalwood skin you've rubbed off on me
making me smooth chocolate,
and you, grained gold damned to greatness.

When you notice me painting, you
stand a little straighter,
pucker a bit more.
Smile and smirk like I've shown you
private things in a crowded room.
You know I like to show out--- only for you.

Merlot sways in the glass of your eyes like you've turned the tables on me.
You've caught me looking and now under your spotlight,
There's no other heat I'd like to receive.

You know I'm comfortable with confrontation baby,
So I don't look away.

I am interactive art.
The type of painting where each stroke touches you;
Old fashions that have you loose and feeling new,
all while moaning a song you've heard as much as your own thoughts;
but every time it plays, is the first time.

I memorize the travel of your eyes,
the basketball bouncing in your throat,
and the deep breaths through your rounded nose with a button
I wish to push with my finger tips.
See, we are finding pieces of each other that feel familiar,
Pieces we know can fit together.
If we want them to.

I remember when my goosebumps travel under the ghosts of your hands,
Your beard itches you to tickle and tense me,
broad shoulders hold your day
but strong and subtle arms interlock,
as if holding each other back from the sinful apple.

Oh baby, don't you judge me
You know wanting you is my vulnerability.
I'm trying to find your secrets in the dips and groves of your melanin,
your Godlike skin;
warred and perfected by life's storms-
your creation is something I see His fingerprints are still on
and my eyes, are still on you.

In Your Element

I remember back when I used to daydream about you,
I'd write you into my day.
I'd sing your name in my favorite songs: *My Love, My Light.*
I made sure I prayed for you every time you streaked across my mind like a high school dare.
The wind breezes your scent past me, and I remember everything that you and nature have in common;
how you bloomed under sunshine
and how you could never be controlled when you rage.
Out of air,
earth,
fire,
and water,
You, my dear storm,
are the element of surprise.

Dear Lover, (I Miss Loving You)

There's a man on his way to Huntsville, Alabama
He's the courier of my heart and fragile parts
And I'm sending them to you for safe keeping.
I hope you find bits of relief in popping the bubble wrap.
I hope it reminds you of the night I left.
Where our tongues, slipping past boundaries, sung the leaver's song
In the lovers key,
Not knowing when we'd harmonize again.

I hope you don't remember the morning,
When you woke up clutching your loneliness and flat pillows,
In a fetal position on the edge of the bed.
Still saving your innermost parts for my return.
I hope you still laughed that day and mourned me as an afterthought.
Made your memories of me a practice rather than a prayer God can repeat back to you.
Every bone in my body hallowed itself and hid your traces;
Storing you for the long way home.

I'd be there if I was selfish enough.
I'd be there if I knew how to tuck my fears behind my ears.
I'd be there just to make your crescent moons smiles in the darkness.
I'd learn the lyrics to the songs you say remind you of me;
And I'd sing them into your ear like a secret.
I want to plant myself in your soil and see what we know about making grass greener.
I'd grow like a weed with you--intertwined and selfish with our energy.
Or, maybe we can grow like sunflowers,
stocky and smiling speckled at the sun.
Defiant and beautiful in our own way,
we'd be the prettiest wild flowers in all Alabama, sho'nuf.
Loving each other with the languages
of the worlds we've traveled.
Knowing it takes time,
knowing it takes a trip,
knowing it takes a chance...
Possibly in a letter or a packaged heart,
found on this random man to Huntsville,
I hope you find him
and find me, loving you---Soon.

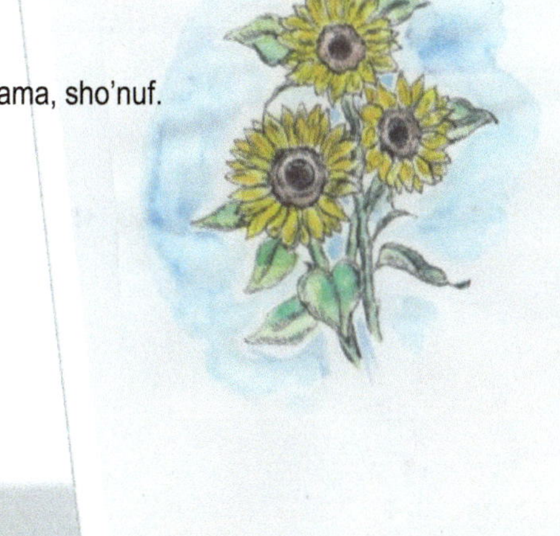

Gravity

You remind me of gravity
and the first time I felt human.
The first sting is as painful as the rest,
your kisses remind me of skinning my knees.
I became another girl gushing blood.
My body is where I've seen the most blood of wars.
Your words remind me of bumping my head on broken promises,
broken hymens...
It all made sense then,
when teeth,
tongue,
fingers
and scars
were made for the same purpose.

A Lesson on Impermanence

Sheets tangled and were washed,
and cold air tasted our exposed skin.
Your tongue, razor sharp with my sweets dripping;
I am still cut,
and dripping.

Your fingerprints on the inside of me,
my makeup was smeared into a forced grin.
Your lips are too swollen to finish what you started,
while my faith is held between my teeth every Sunday
in the form of hymns and raised hands...
You pulled me a part vein by vein
just to fit yourself inside
of somewhere you never meant to claim.

Who knew your silence could be a weapon?
Who knew scars could form the best memories?
But in time, they fade.
And in time you'll break.
Trickling down into an urn on my nightstand.
You are everything I've never learned to lose-
you are made of promise, and the things I let slip through my hands.

A Summoning of the Family, Through Recipe Rituals

For My Grandma Crockett

Start by cutting your onions, celery, and pepper.
Deshell four cloves of garlic.
My hands start to clam and hover around the knife's base
And I hear my grandma whisper "be patient, take it easy, don't rush".
When the white onions sting my eyes and make me cry, I let them.
This is the first time I've heard her voice since she died.
But it doesn't sound like a memory,
Maybe this ritual of making her stew brings her to me
As she is now.
Maybe she sees me, as I've grown to be, now.

Toss the garlic cloves and a scotch bonnet into a boiling pot, let it steam and murmur with the water, just for flavor, just for taste.
Take your beef and put it in flour, then hot oil in a pan, brown your meat so it will tenderize in the stew.
I hear her giggle sizzling on all sides.
She says "there you go baby, don't let the flour burn".
I wonder if she's seen my flowers burn.
On the days I am not fit to be anyone's legacy, does she turn her head from my body of smoke signals or does she say, "you blaze wonderfully, the way I used to.
When I was your age.
Untamed, the wild widened me until I burst.
Granddaughter—become unashamed of being insatiable.
Perfume floats into your sanctuary from your altar, and they adorn you.
There are millions of candles on altars inside of us—one for each prayer, and each breath, let them swell. Light a million more for your daughters.
Teach them to pray and carry the family with them".

As the meat browns, put it in the boiling pot.
From that create a broth. Let them tenderize, and break apart.
Let us break apart. Always caught in these selfish offerings.
I don't know whether hearing her voice in my ear,
feeling her hand weigh on my head as if she is still taller than me,
or feeling her laugh on my back is somewhere in a middle passage between life and death.

Is she called to my offerings?
Is she attached to the big bellied pot?
Is the okra a portal that conjures her memories of living?

She tells me to move on to the heart of this altar.
The spices, the fire, the ladles we use to taste all drip on the side of the pot.
She is here now.
She lets me stir.
She gives me the space to taste and pour until I remember.
Until I see her in every layer of this pot.
Until the scotch bonnet bursts from the heat, she pops like a bubblegum bored child.
We add the chopped veggies, the flour, tomato paste, the meat stew,
Worcestershire sauce, hot sauce, potatoes, old bay, bay leaves, okra, salt, sugar, cayenne, crushed peppers,
We fill the pot to the top and fall into a hushed hum—we are in sync; neither death or life between us.
We are in realms where we can see each other's eyes—
not as they were but as we are, now.
She takes the spoon and swirls spices and prayers about,
with the family hunching over her.
All of them have come now.
She tastes and smiles like a million heard prayers, a million answered.
My father kisses my forehead with oneness.
Who knew some family reunions could only occur in a séance.
Of all the family traditions—he smiles like he never wanted to witness this from the other side.
Lord knows I wanted him to teach me the things I wait to love about myself—
But for now, he touches my mother's hand.
She says she feels a chill, and hugs the blanket closer to her shoulders—
'Is it ready'?
It is momma.
I am one with the hosts of family here.
And oh, how we serve each other, the feast of this life.

Moonlight (For my dad, brother, nephew, husband, and future sons)

Where do black boys go when they go quiet?
Where do they go to feel like pain won't last?
As the serenity of the moon serenades their souls
they are reborn,
diamonds glistening off their skin...
Where do black boys go when they're tired of sinning
and are they overcome by that darkness;
where the sweetest of berries are strangled into wine
sipped at dinner time by idolized crime and crack babies cryin'...

Where do their dreams go when they die,
do they sag into memories like fertilizer in graves,
or do they reload into cop burners;
bullets quick and fleeting like visions
like news coverage,
and like construction on gentrified housing
quick and fleeting like black lives?

Forbidden fruit falls from black wombs-
too ethereal for earth, and too human for heaven.
Black boys learn not to cry when they look death in the eye,
they'd rather die swinging
than let someone pull their card or swipe their chain.
Black boys learn to die for trivial things,
or things they should already own like divinity and dignity.
And planted seeds of knowledge.

They are hung from the trees that press sacred script
and don't publish their obituaries,
but we call it education;
black boys are killed for knowing-
knowing how to beat the system,
how to leave the system
and not love the street corners that feed from the system.

The system is the grit of greed
and the threat is real;
as real as the streets they rep,
the blood they bleed
and the niggas they kill.
Where do black boys go to get away from it all,
do they welcome the stillness or fight these unfamiliar stirrings?

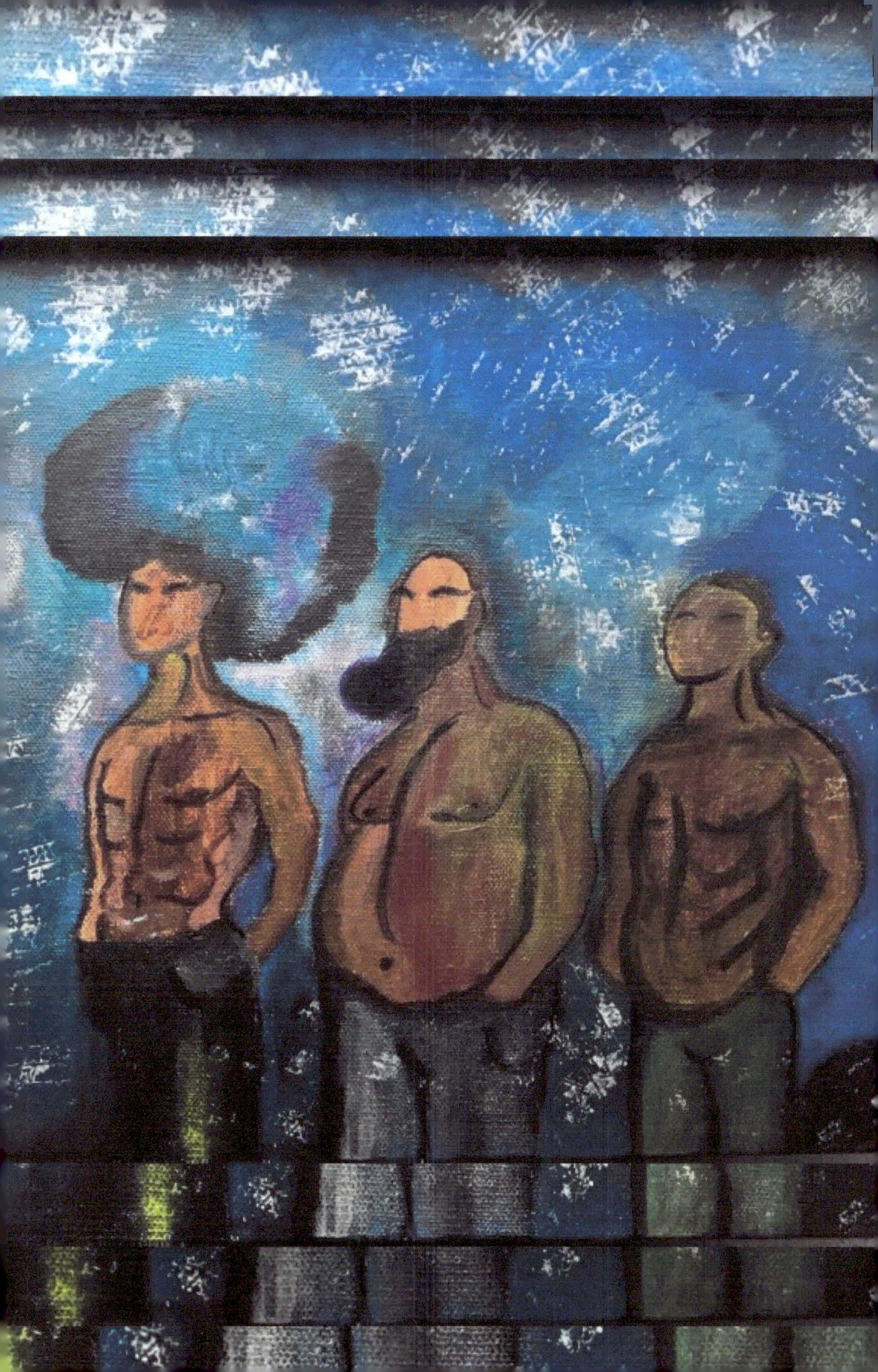

God’s Kin

God must have kinfolk, and she must be skinfolk,
because I see her every day.
She is pulled from rib, it’s the first cage she’d ever seen with her own eyes.
She is caged by religion talk and man’s weakness.
She sometimes wonders if they are one in the same,
they chain the same and clink in tune.

These chains remind her of gravity
and the issues of blood in her family.
They spill over like wine on carpets,
they cry over the holes in their stories
and laugh with broken teeth.
She smiles like she shouldn’t; like her secrets are dirty
and she wonders if God sees her secrets and calls her dirty.
Or, does he call her by her name, still?

Does God watch over the black women that raise sons with holes like Jesus?
Does he give them a bosom to rest their head and a cross to rest their sins?

She sits with me when God goes to church,
she oils my scalp and teaches me scripture.
We watch honey bees glaze and glide over petals…
They too, are the laborers that hold nature’s beauty by its’ seams.
I hide her in my heart and she slides into the pews of my prayers;
she is not religion nor the sin of man.
She is the tangible spirit,
the same spirit Thomas felt when he touched Jesus’ hands
and doubted no more.
She tells me I am the color purple that God made so he can never take his eyes off me-
she reminds me I am the lily planted in the valley.
Her voice is rain on my skin,
I chose her as my kin;
we have found healing and redemption where no one expected it to live.
It now lives in me.

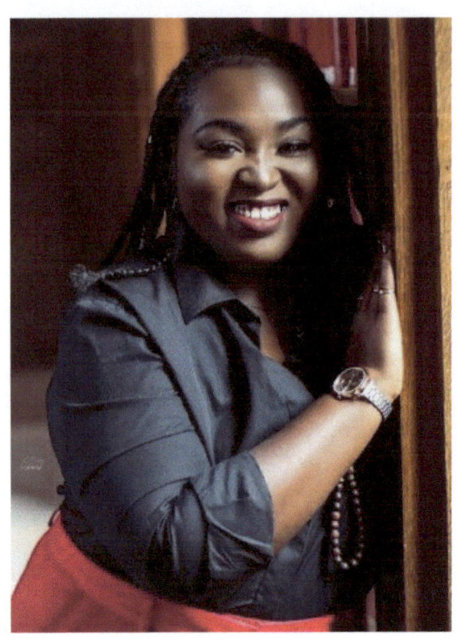

About the Author

Briana Crockett is a womanist, a proud and talented black feminist. She is also a poet, self- established artist and spiritual woman who identifies strongly with black and spiritual culture and values. Born and raised in Boston and a recent graduate of English, Music and African American Studies at Bridgewater State University, this young author is deeply inspired by authentic connections and soul bonds. Briana believes in the power of love, and that the greatest gift one could both give and receive is love.

Briana *loves* creating art through multiple mediums and believes that art is energy; it morphs and transitions through various mediums and channels. We humans are channels- conduits for the imagination, spirit, and a higher consciousness to shine through.

In her free time, Briana enjoys people watching, binging on reality tv, doing hair, eating good food, going to open mics, writing poetry, and vibing to great music. Her debut book, "*The Growing Place*," is both a recollection of her own life experience and inspired by all she has witnessed in her communities. Writing has been a love of hers since finding her groove. She is further inspired by the power and importance of *soul mate* love- how we have multiple soul ties to not only people, but to places, sacred objects and natural environments. Briana is interested in explaining, questioning and strengthening the ties which connect us to our humanity and time. (Time in a multi- dimensional, non- linear and eternal sense!)

Briana was the president of her college poetry club, has had her poetry published at various stages of her life since 4th grade, and has aspirations of being a successful writer with a potential radio show. She has had many visions of creating world- class music combined with spoken word poetry, and finally knows strongly within that her life purpose and soul calling involves performance, music and poetry.

Briana can be contacted for artistic or poetic requests at: ***bcrockett22@outlook.com***
Simultaneously, her blog/website can be seen here: ***bybriana.com***

www.ingramcontent.com/pod-product-compliance
Lightning Source LLC
LaVergne TN
LVHW052300100826
845147LV00001B/103

* 9 7 8 0 5 7 8 6 3 6 4 3 6 *